MUSICIANS INSTITUTE

PRIVATE LESSONS

Rock
HANON

By Peter Deneff

for
George V. Deneff

ISBN 0-634-06440-1

HAL•LEONARD®
CORPORATION
7777 W. BLUEMOUND RD. P.O. BOX 13819 MILWAUKEE, WI 53213

In Australia Contact:
Hal Leonard Australia Pty. Ltd.
22 Taunton Drive P.O. Box 5130
Cheltenham East, 3192 Victoria, Australia
Email: ausadmin@halleonard.com

Visit Hal Leonard Online at
www.halleonard.com

About the author

Peter Deneff is a pianist, composer, and teacher in Southern California. He began playing at age three and started his formal training at nine with classical pianist Leaine Gibson. He began jazz studies in 1986 with pianist Mike Garson. He studied composition at California State University Long Beach with Dr. Justus Matthews and Dr. Martin Herman. He is currently earning his masters degree in music composition at CSULB, doing studio work, recording discs for the Yamaha Disklavier piano, composing, studying and writing film scores, and performing with his band Excursion as well as with other groups. He also teaches privately and at Cypress College. He resides in Southern California with his wife Diane, and his children Gitana, George, and Sophia.

Introduction

When originally presented with the idea of composing piano exercises in a Rock music style, I immediately began churning over ideas about how to approach the matter. To me, Rock piano playing had always seemed to be more about the "feel" and less about the technique of the pianist. In fact, most of the pioneers of the genre (Jerry Lee Lewis, Fats Domino, Little Richard) were either self taught or had very little formal training. However, this does not imply that Rock piano is simple or void of specific techniques. Therefore, it was necessary to identify those specific difficulties in the style and exploit them through the exercises in this book. The main techniques, which I employed in these studies, are:

- Rapidly repeated chords
- Ostinato bass lines
- Syncopated rhythms
- Pentatonic riffs

While these exercises are certainly difficult and should be practiced as seriously as the original book by C.L. Hanon, they were intended to be enjoyable as well. Try practicing them with a drum machine, sequencer or metronome. I am sure they will be as entertaining to play, as they were to compose. Here are some tips to help you get the most out of your practice session:

- Back should be straight with shoulders relaxed.
- Hands should be low profile with fingers curved.
- Always practice with a metronome, sequencer or drum machine.
- Tempo should be as fast as the exercise can be performed *accurately*.
- Playing should be clean and even.
- Don't forget to breathe!
- Make it groove.

Remember, always keep your practice routine positive and don't forget that you must always enjoy the process of "getting there". As a musician, I don't feel that there is ever an end to the learning process. Therefore, we must embrace that process in order to feel happy and successful in our musical progress. I feel this book will take you to new levels of proficiency and provide months of challenging material to keep you motivated.

Happy playing!
Peter Deneff

1

2

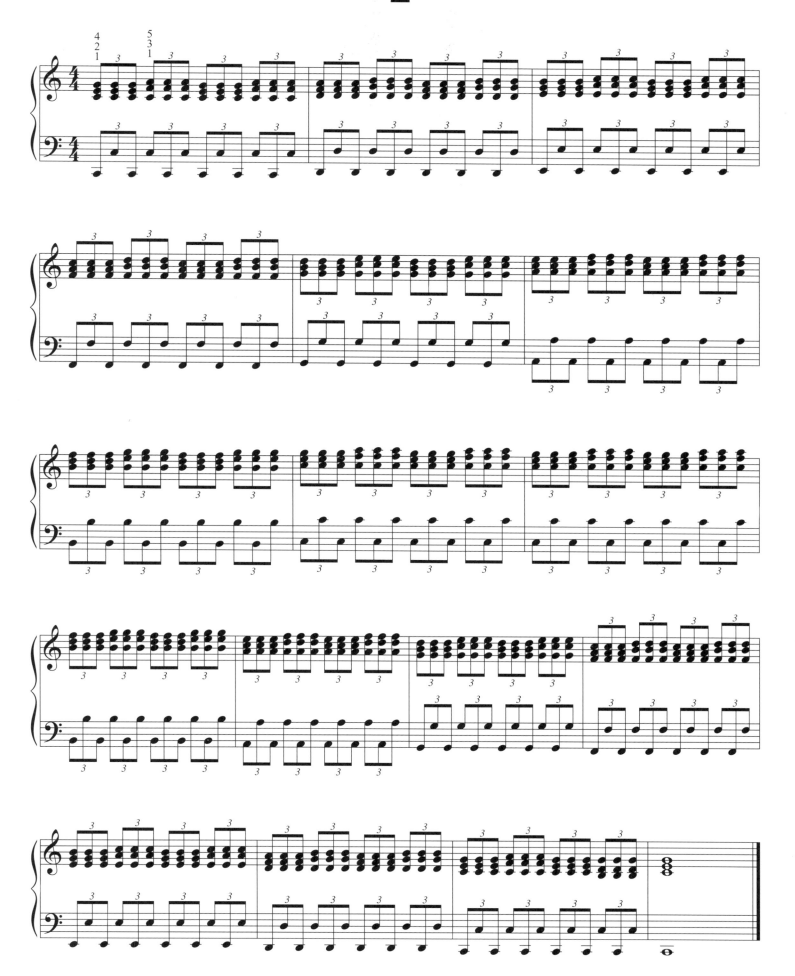

3

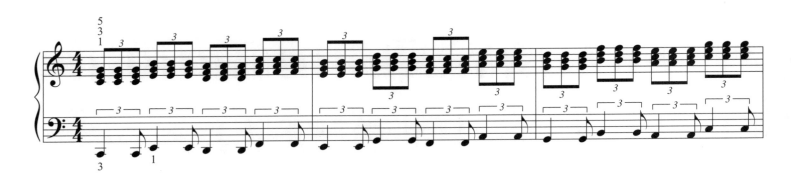

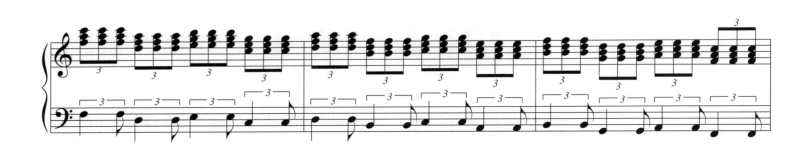

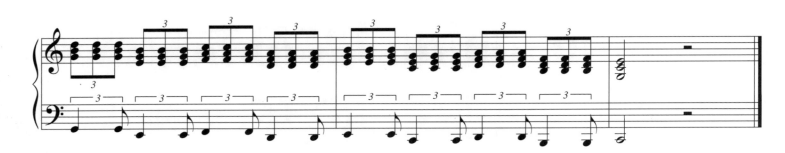

4

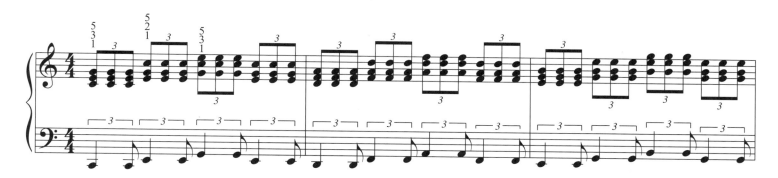

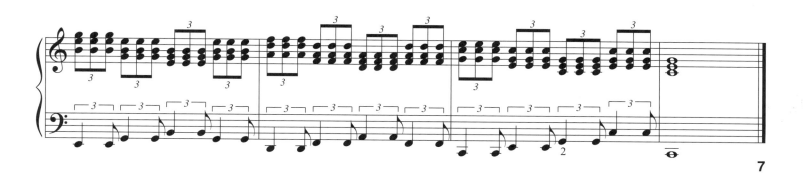

5

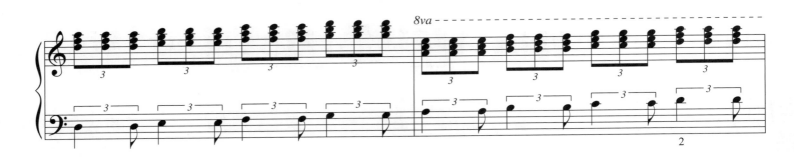

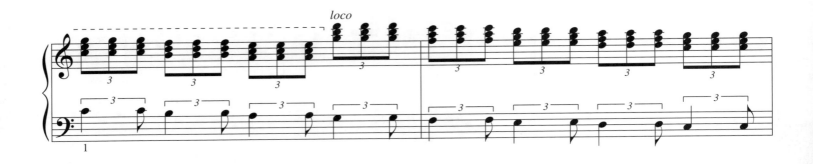

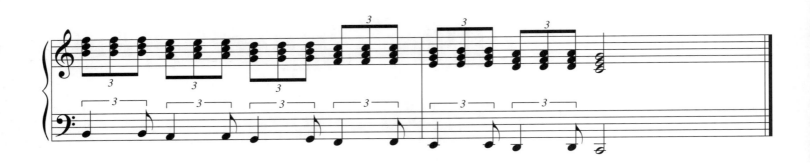

6

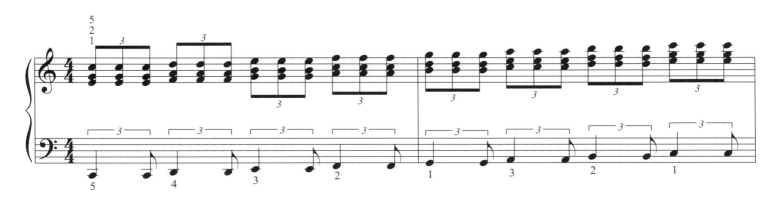

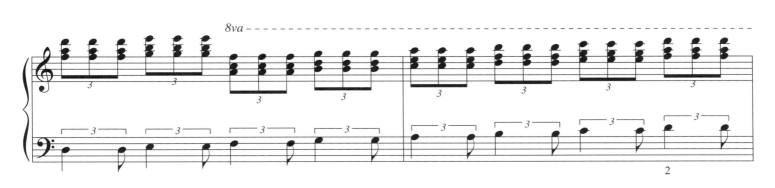

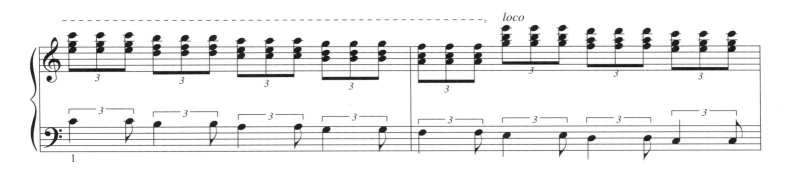

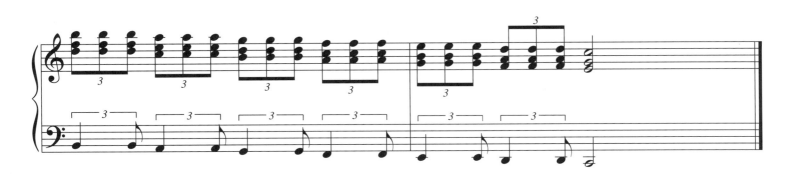

7

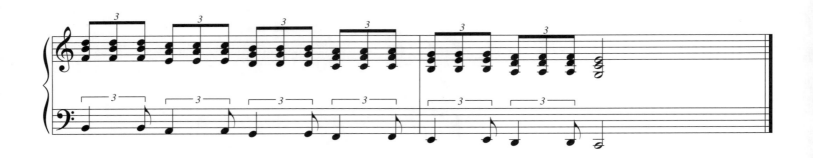

8

9

10

11

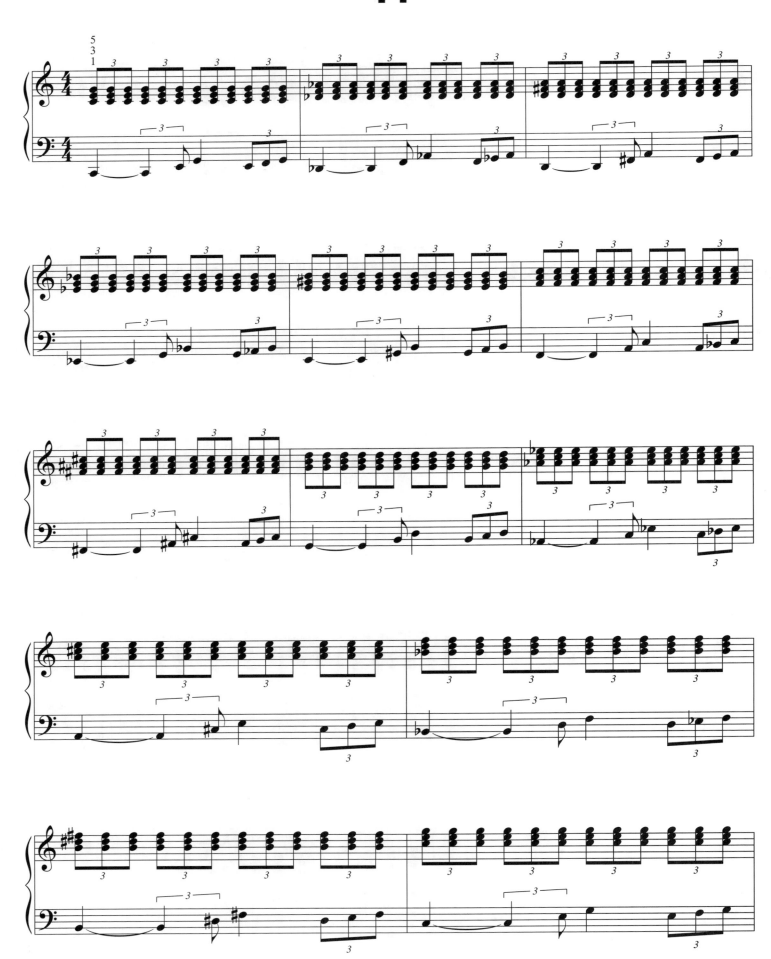

12

13

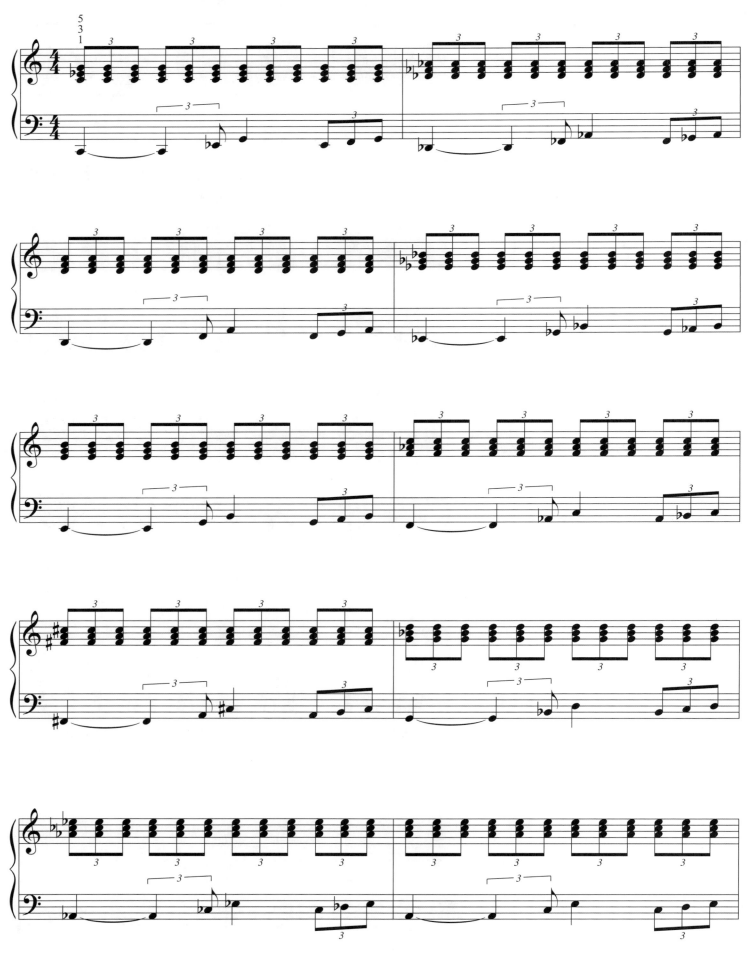

14

15

16

17

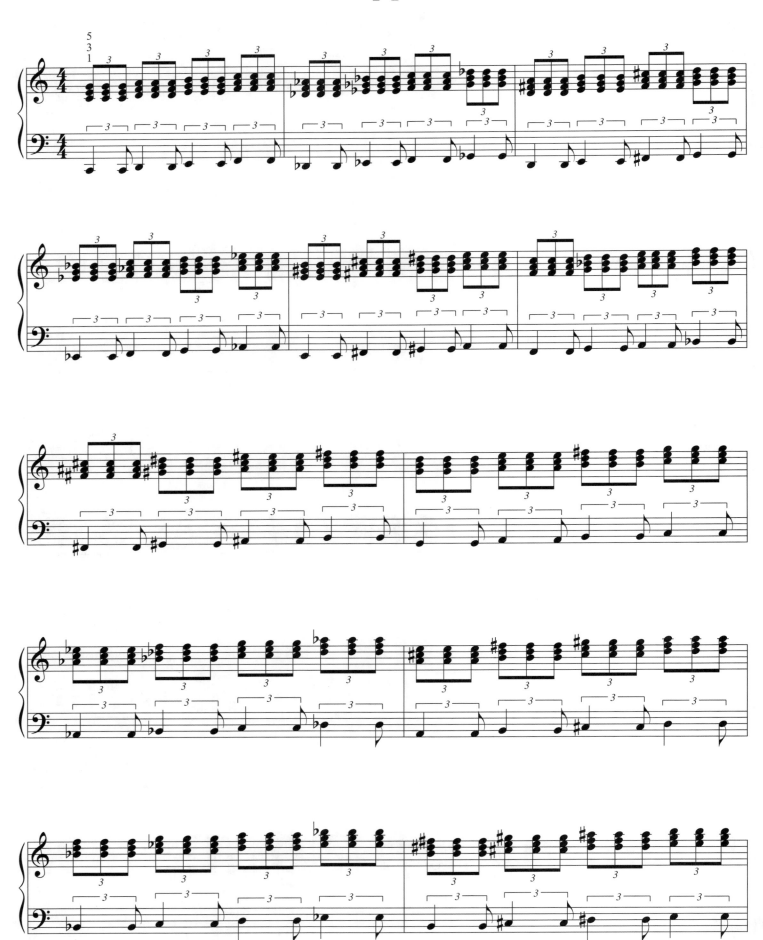

18

19

20

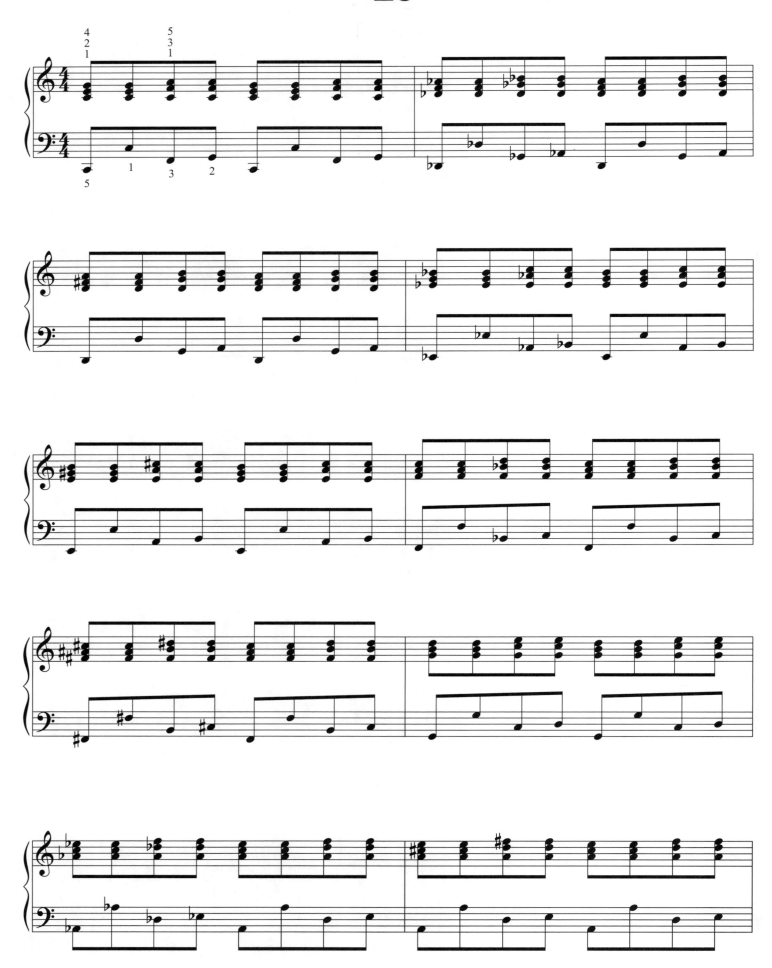

33

21

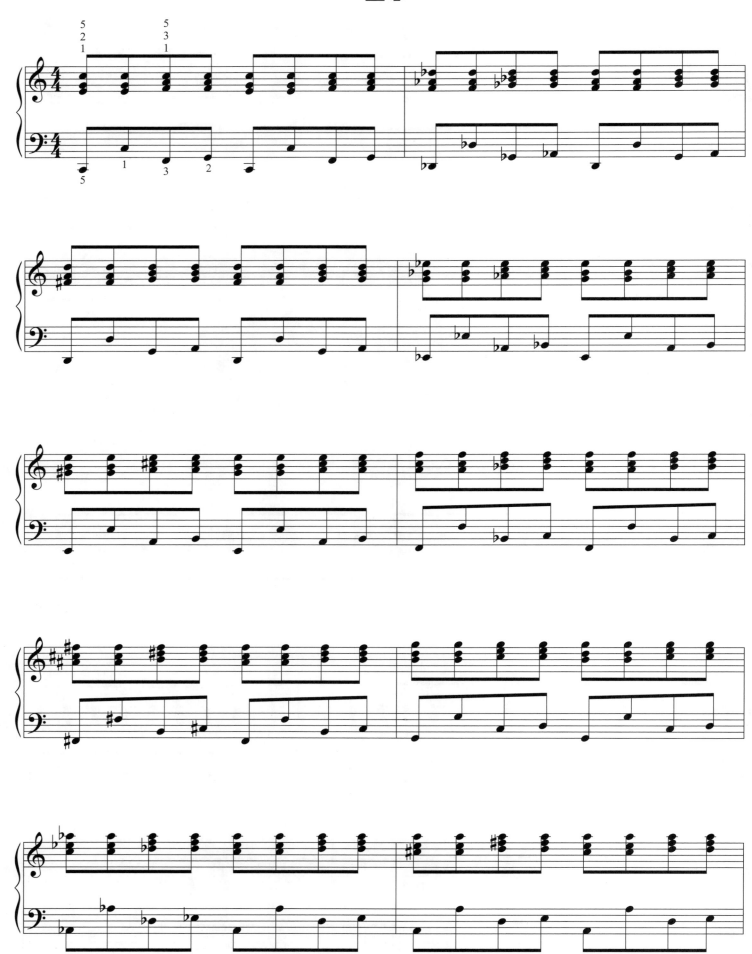

22

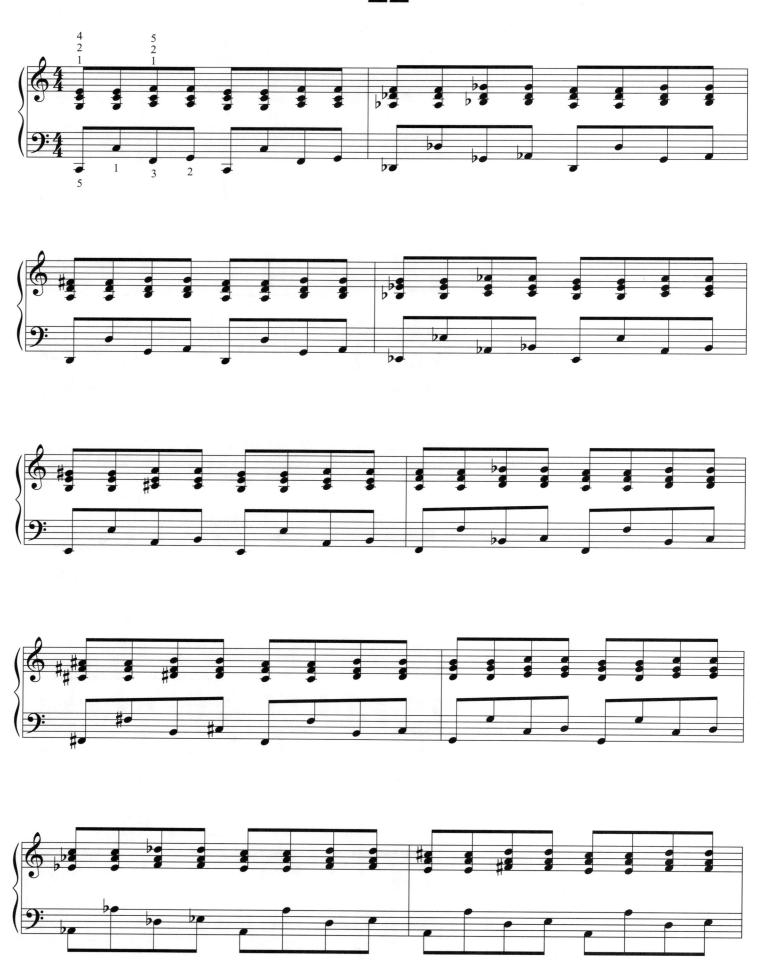

23

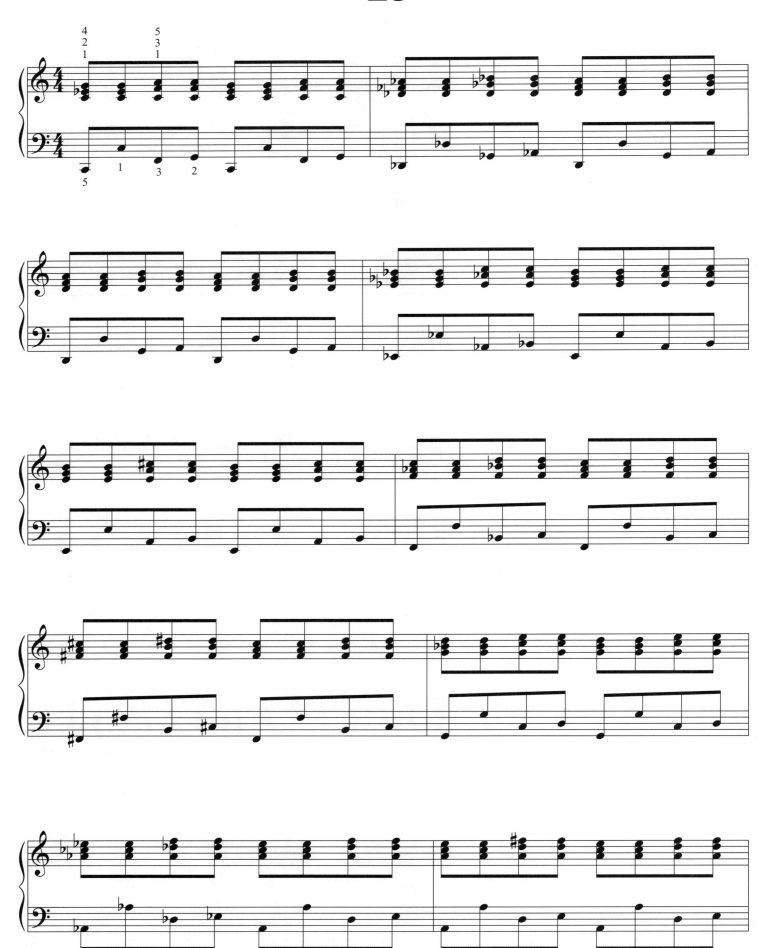

24

41

25

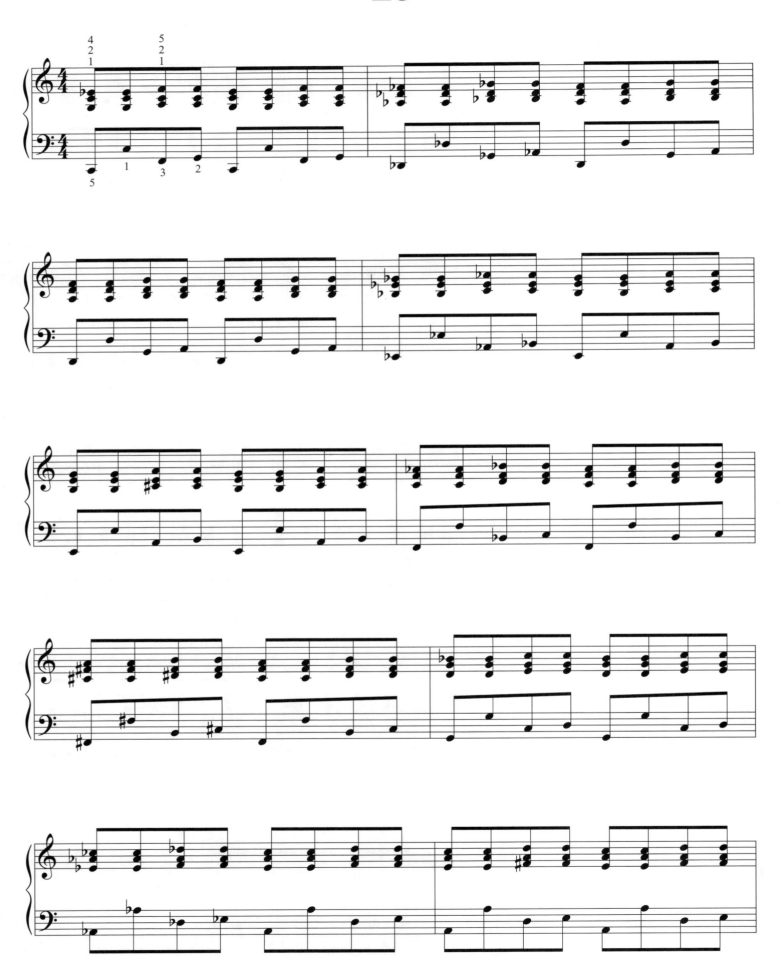

26

27

28

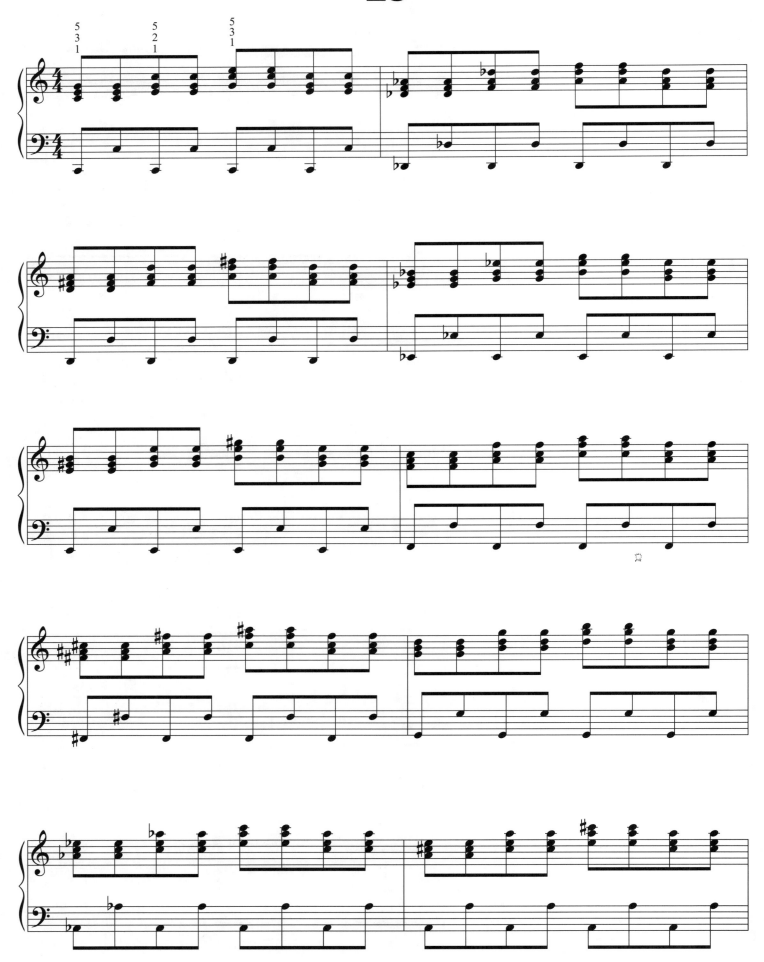

29

30

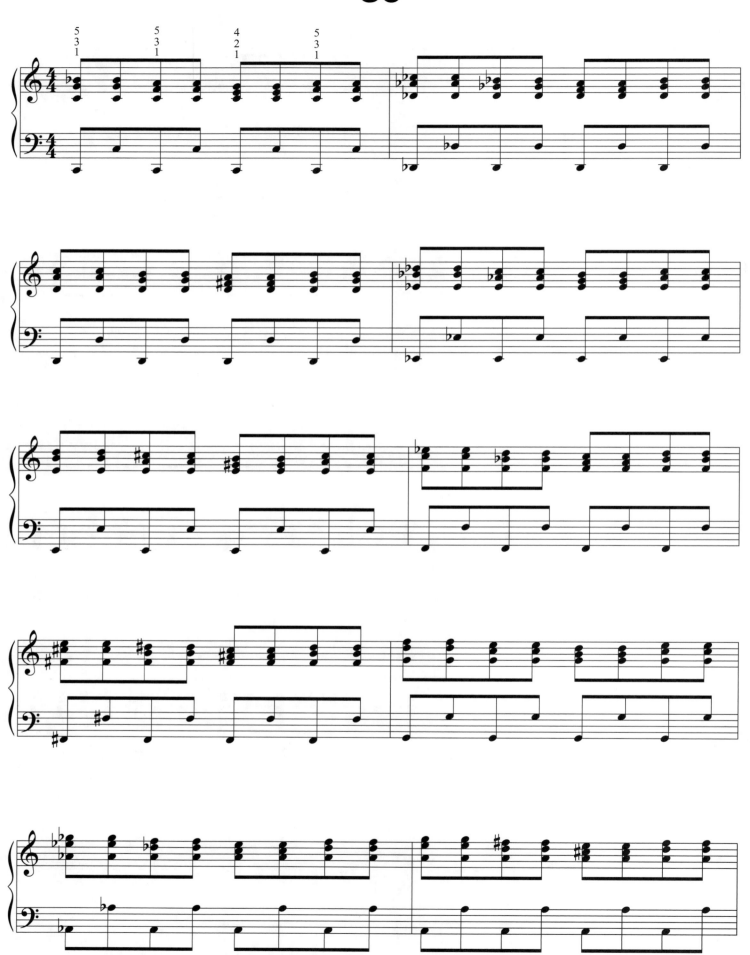

31

32

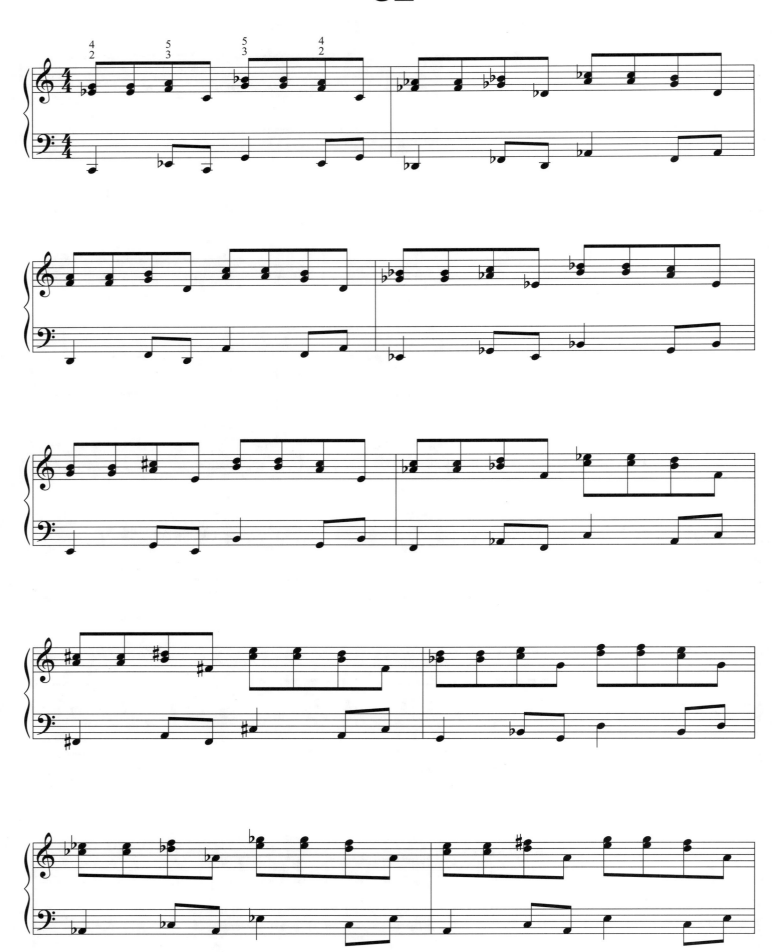

33

59

34

35

36

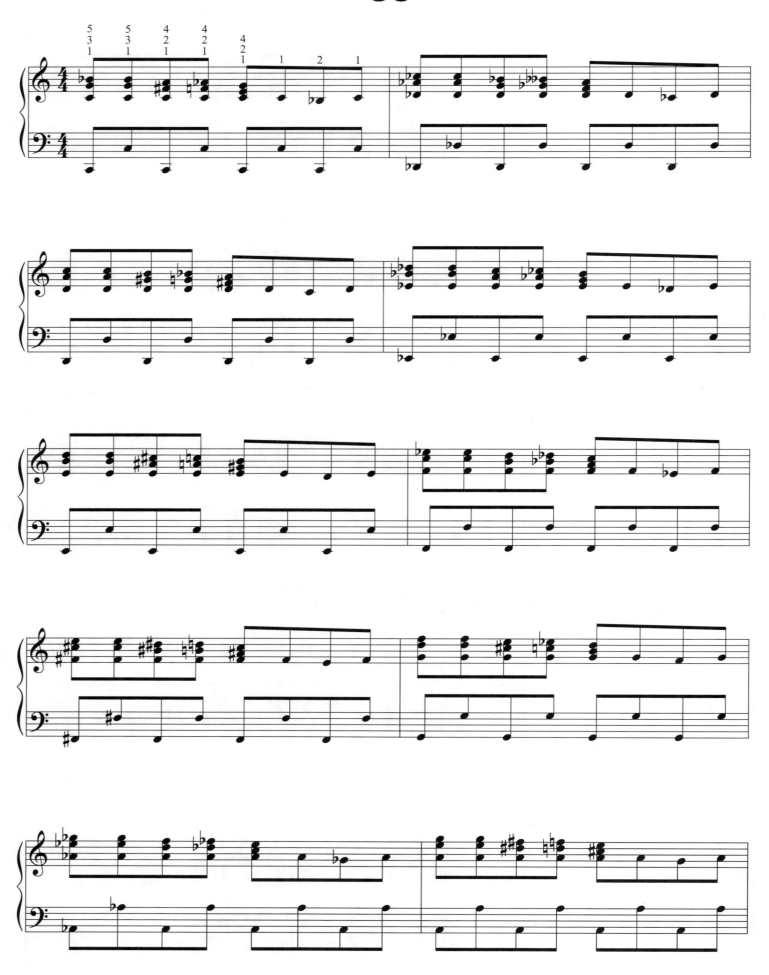

37

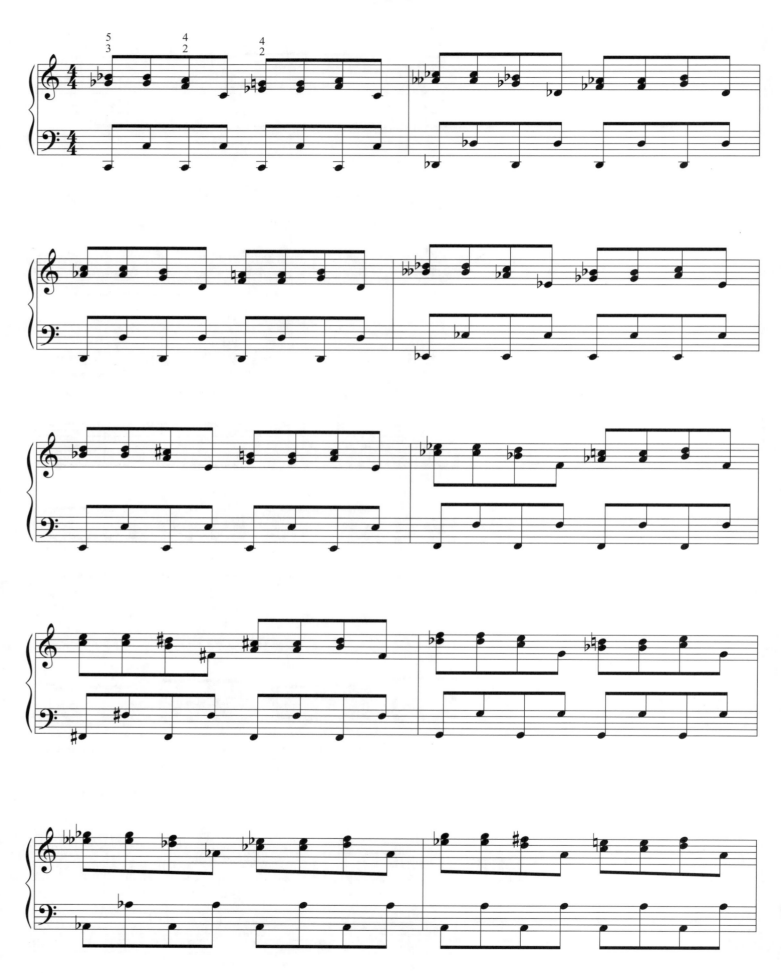

38

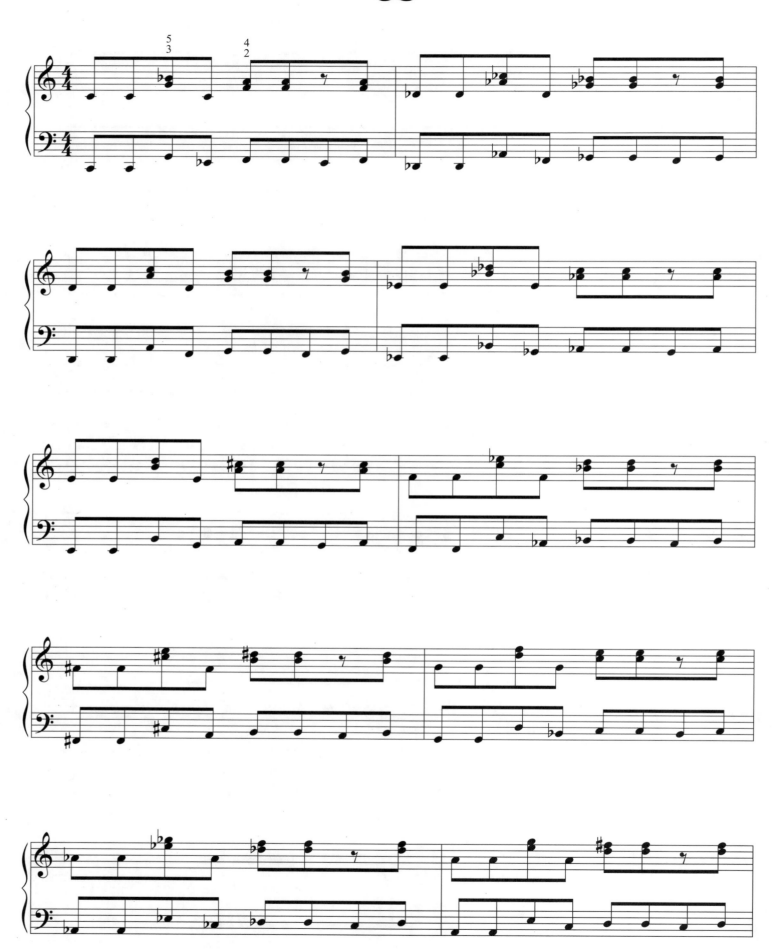

39

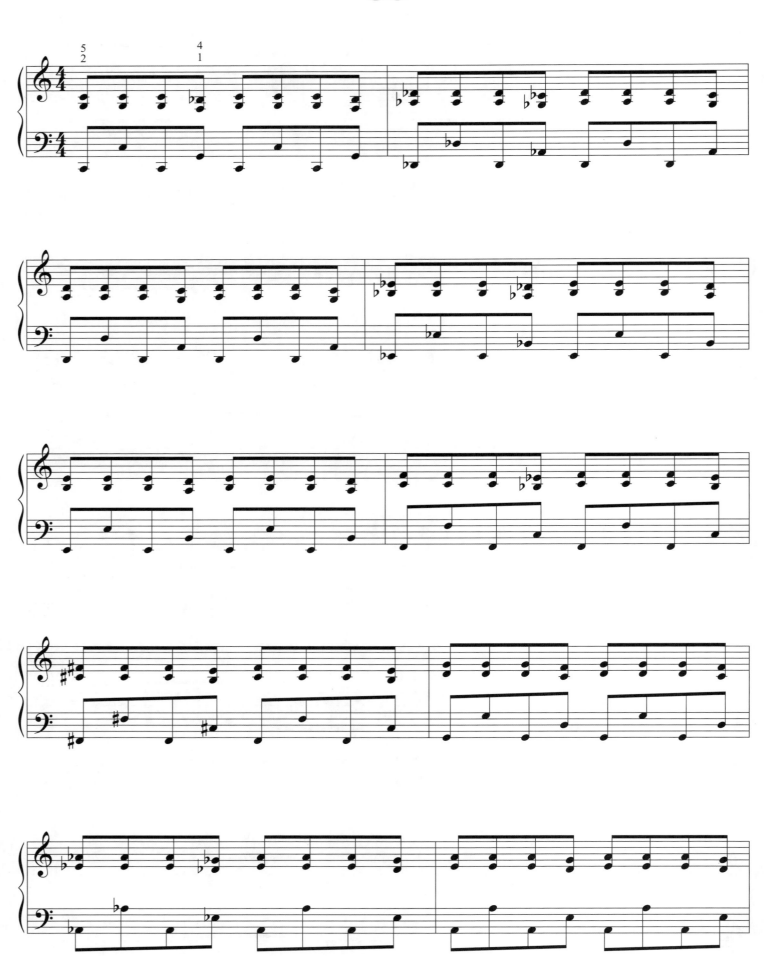

40

41

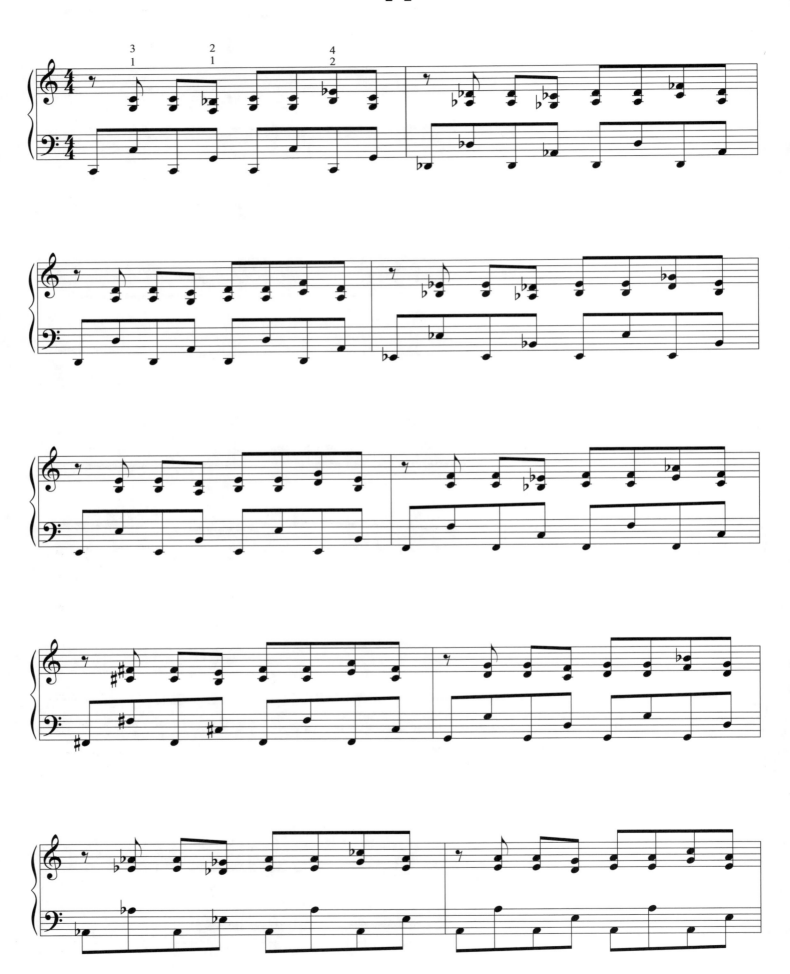

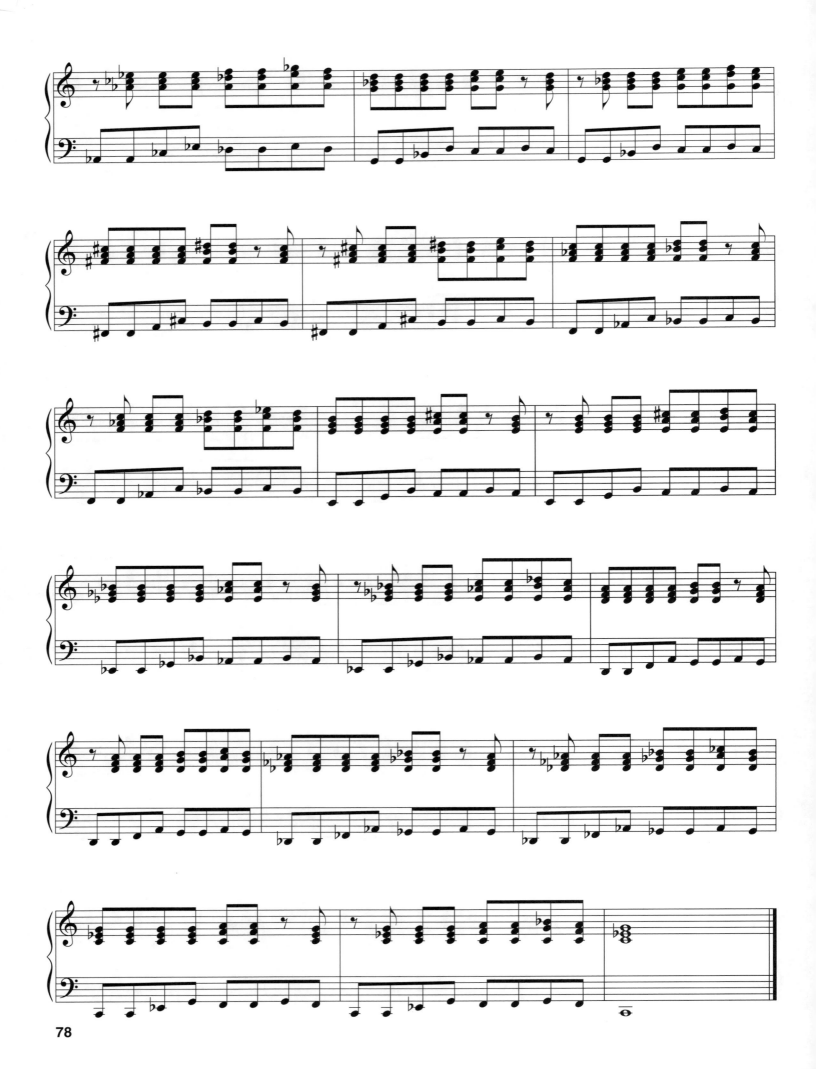

43

44

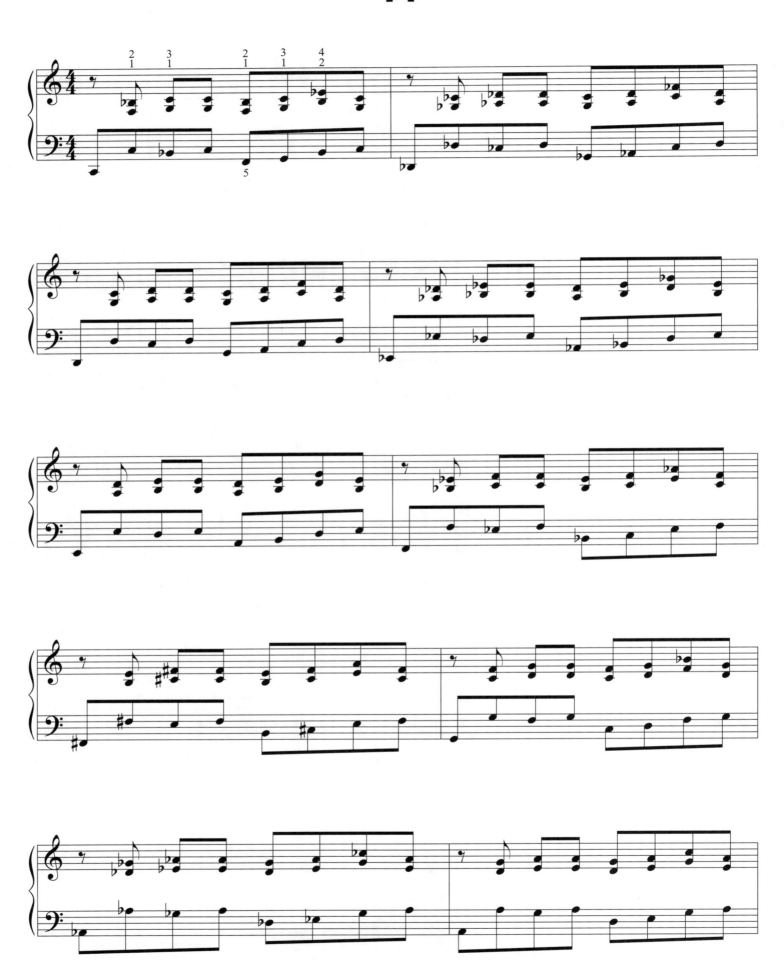

45

46

89

47

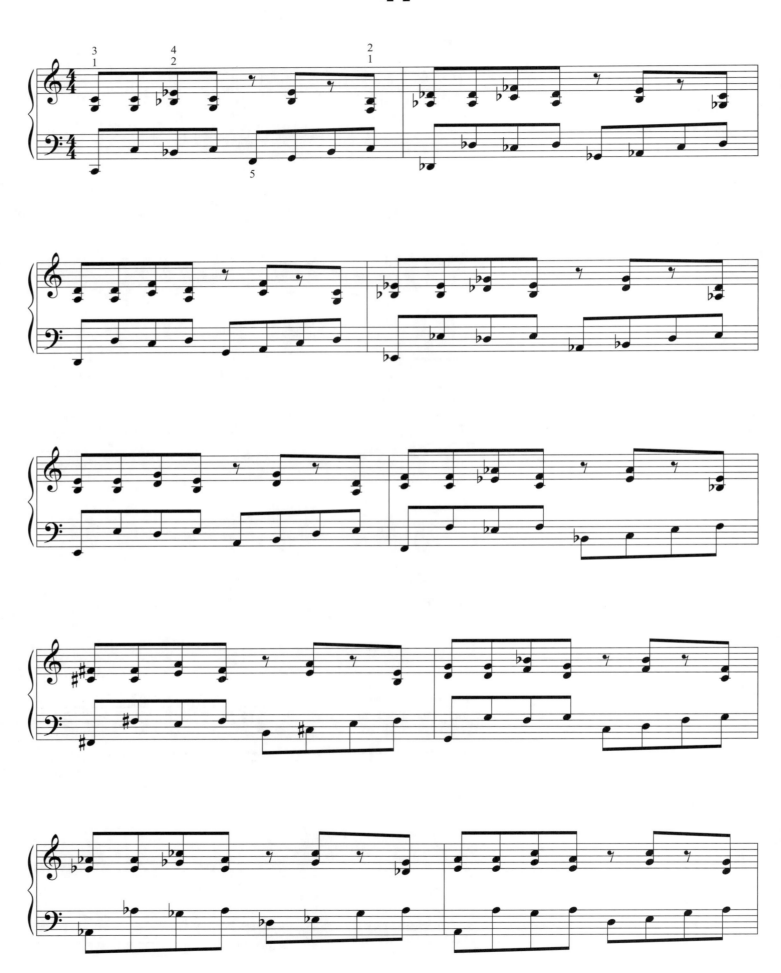

91

48

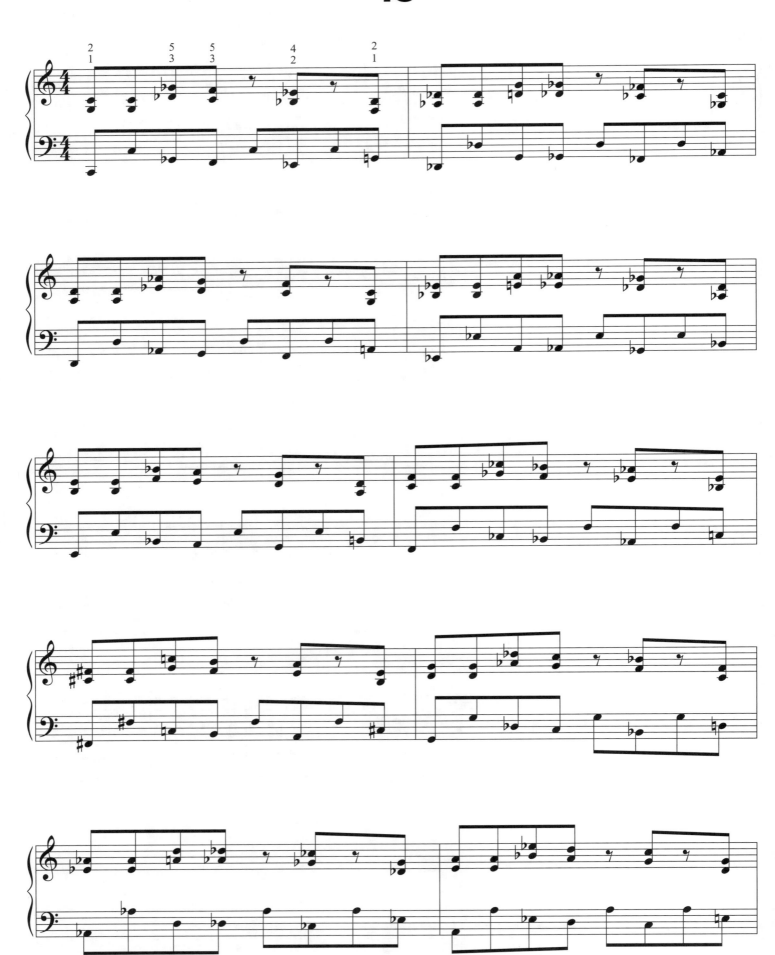

49

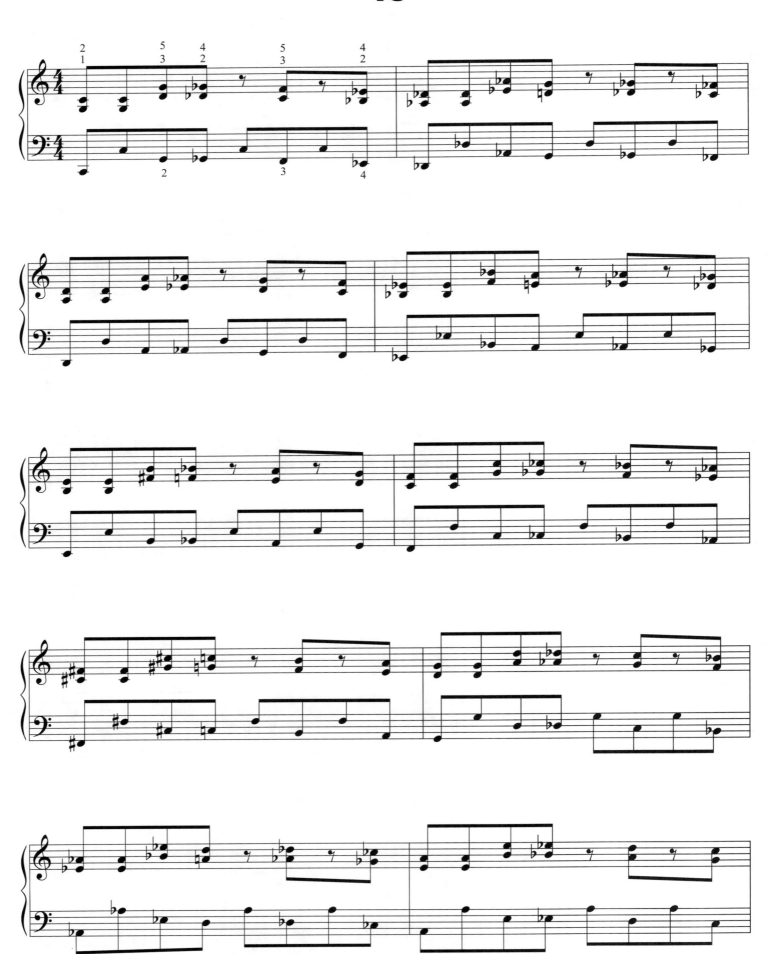

95

50

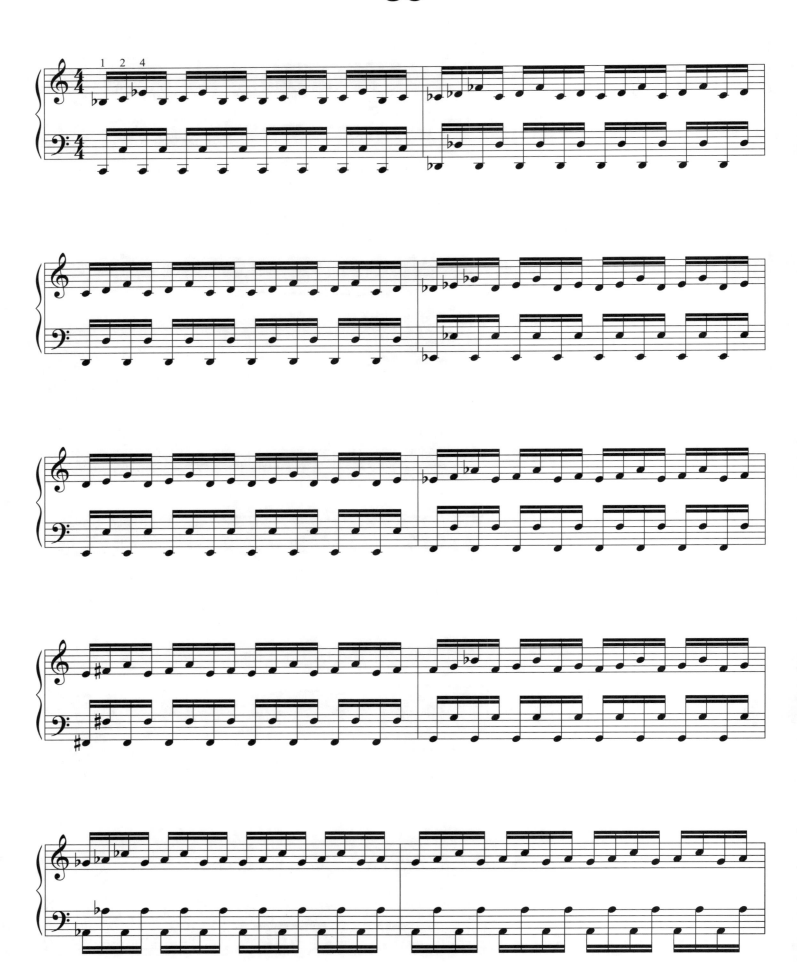

51

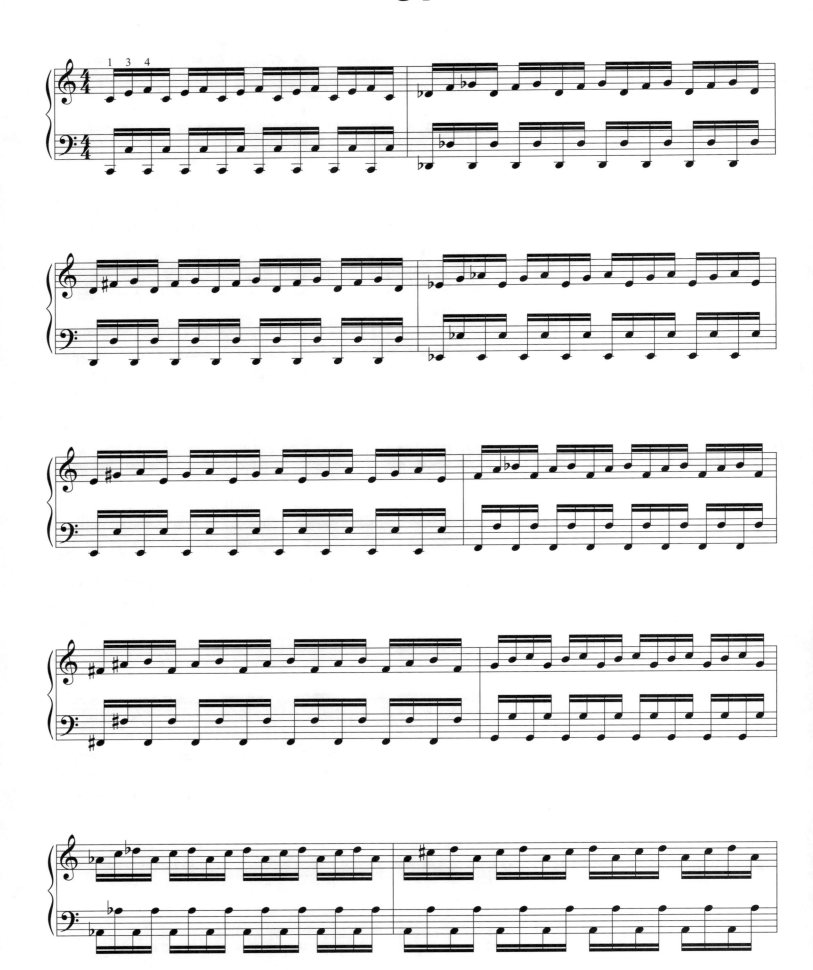

52

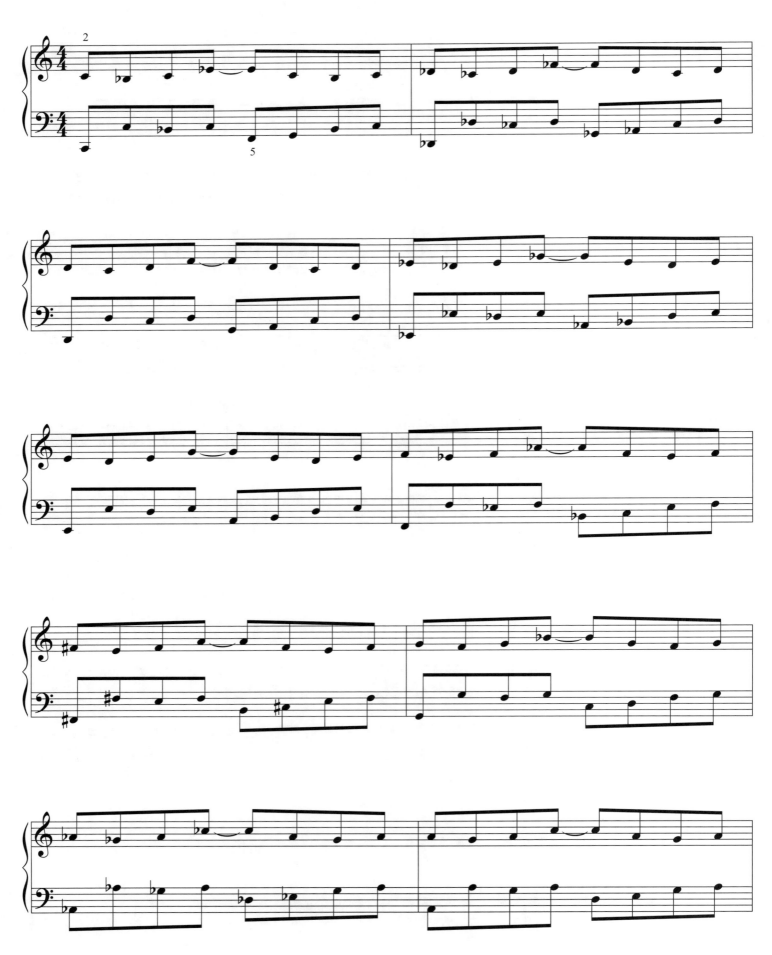

53

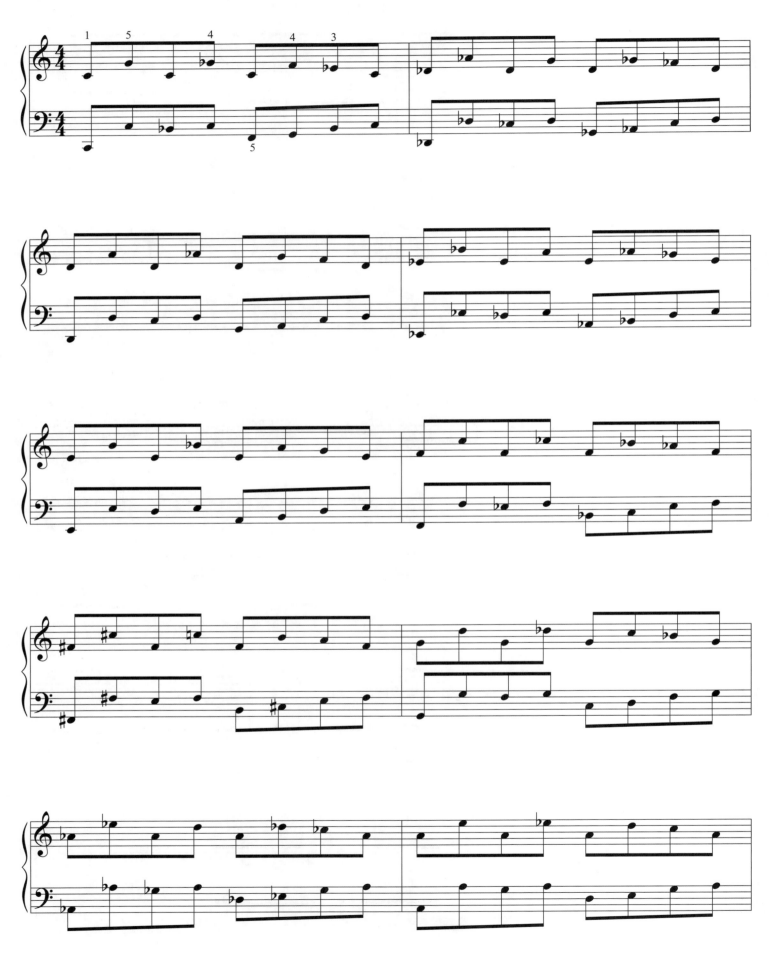

54

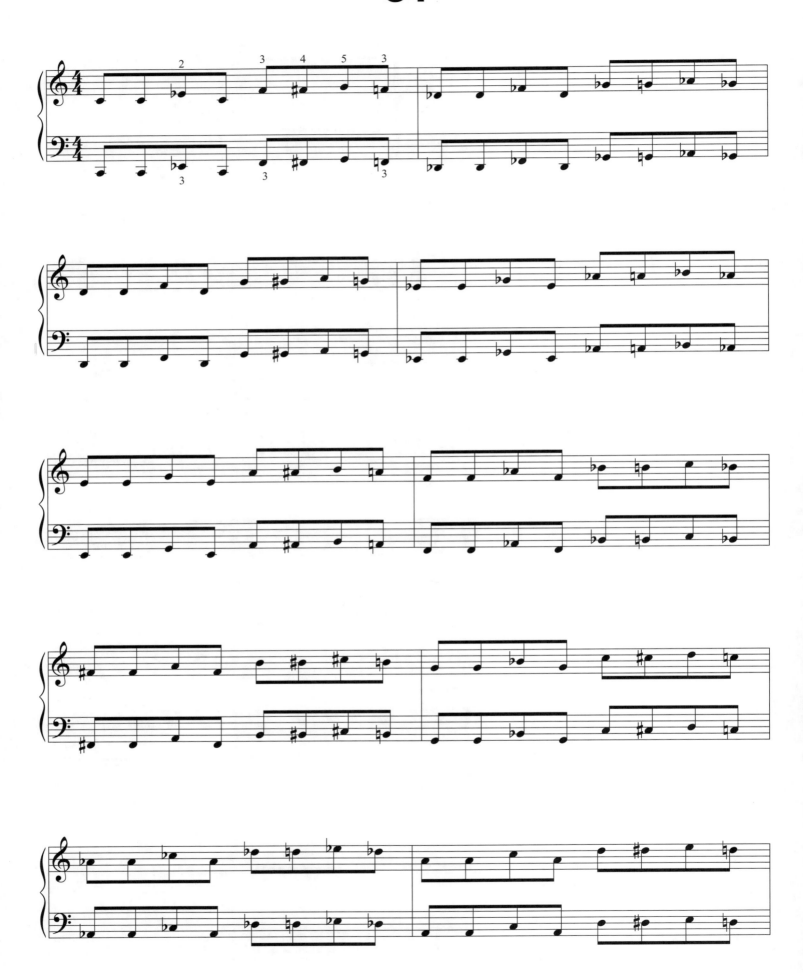

55

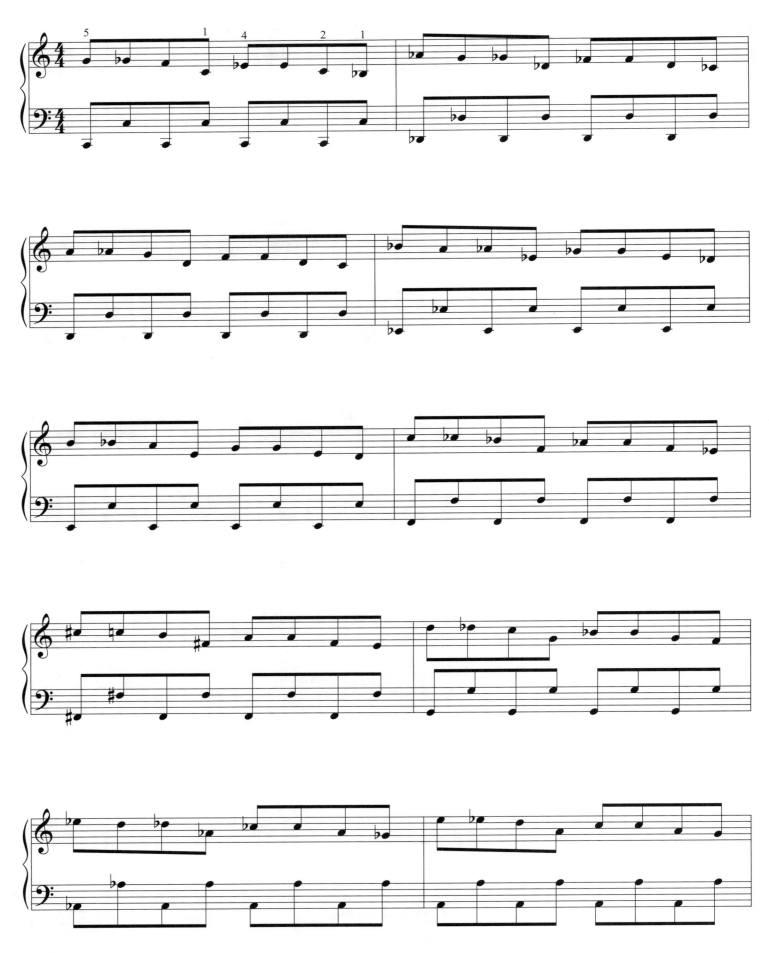

56

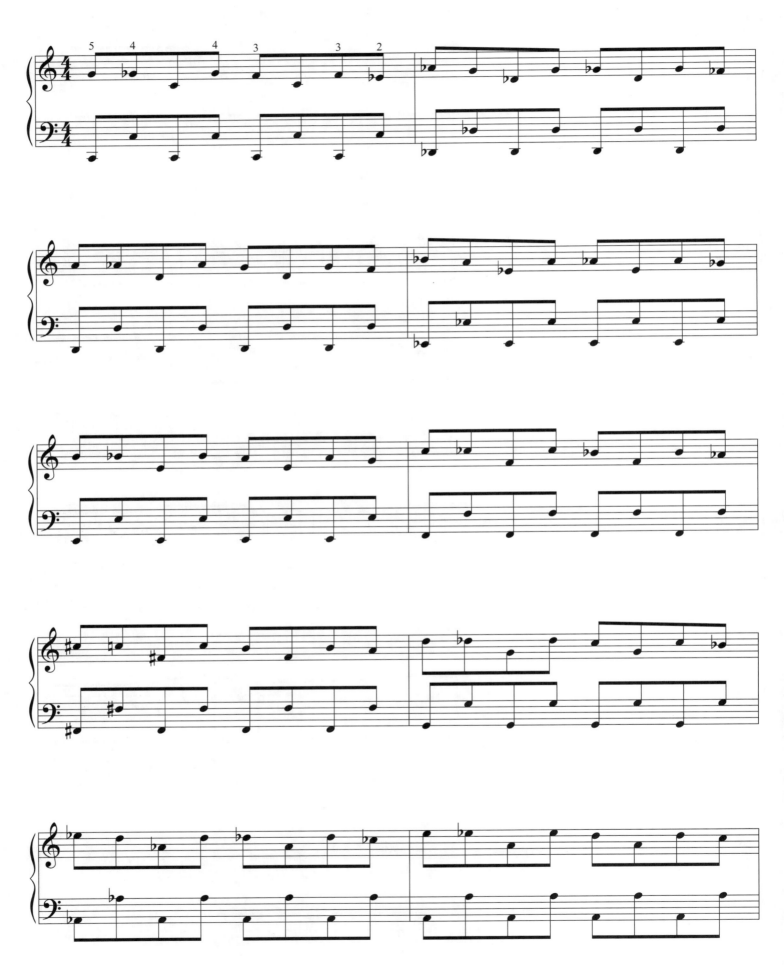

57

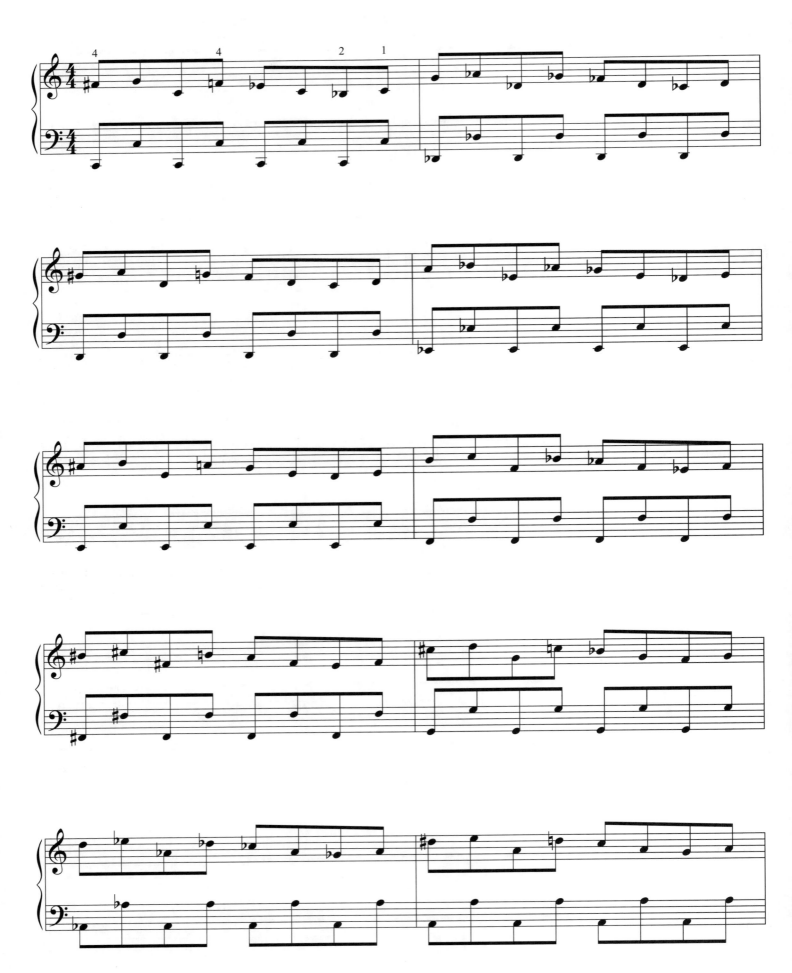

111

58

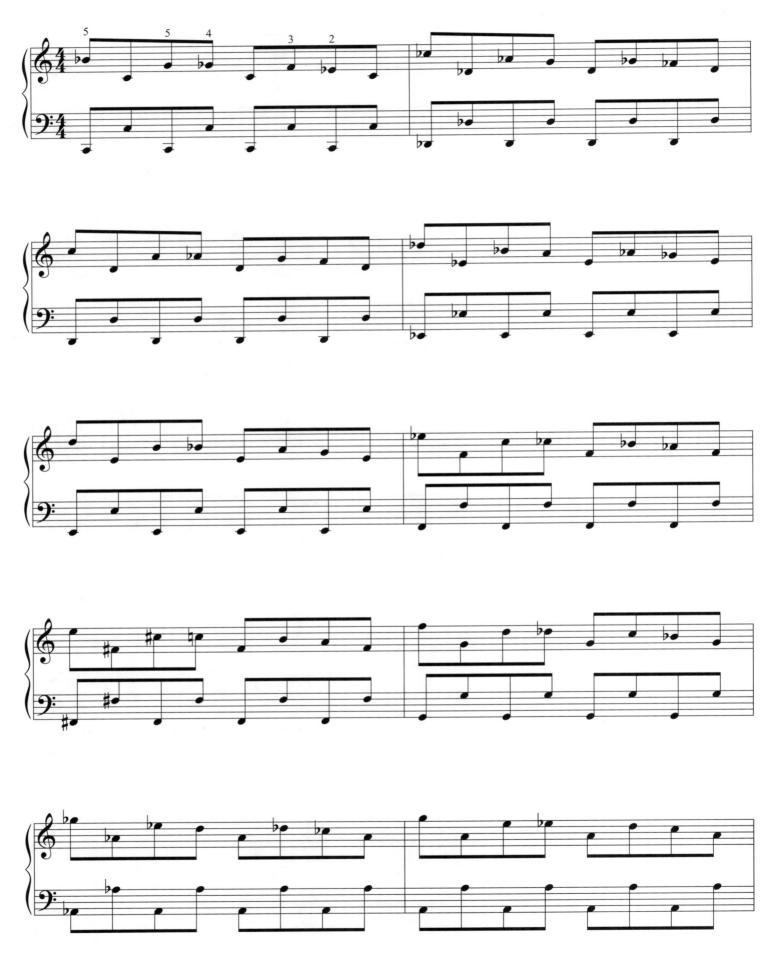

59

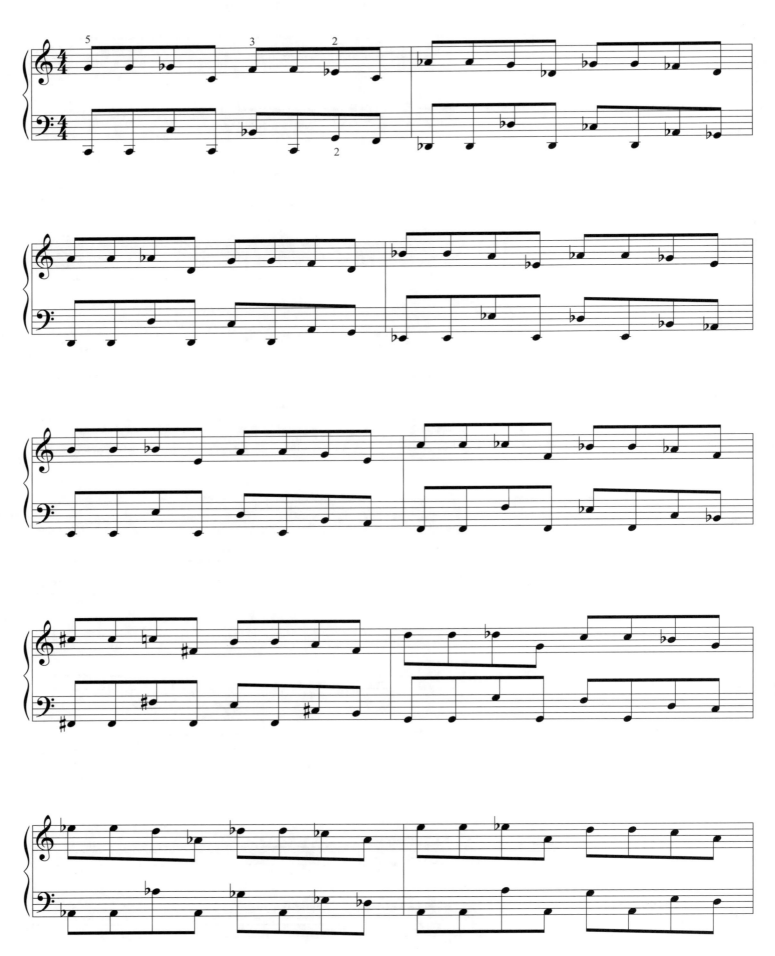

60

117

61

119

62

63

64

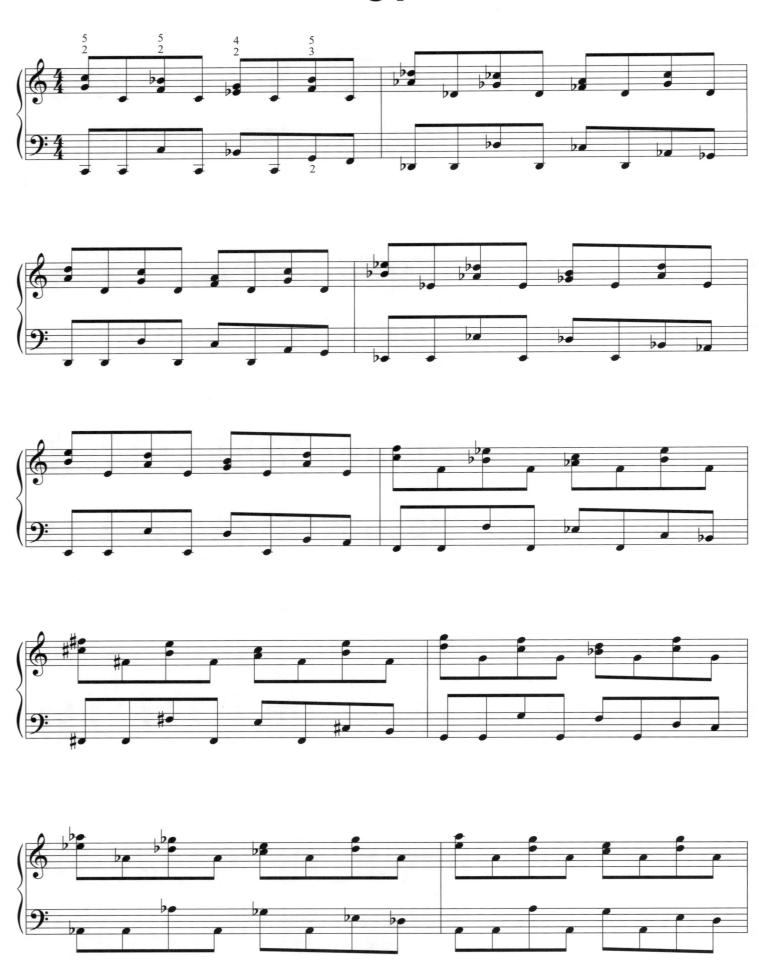

65

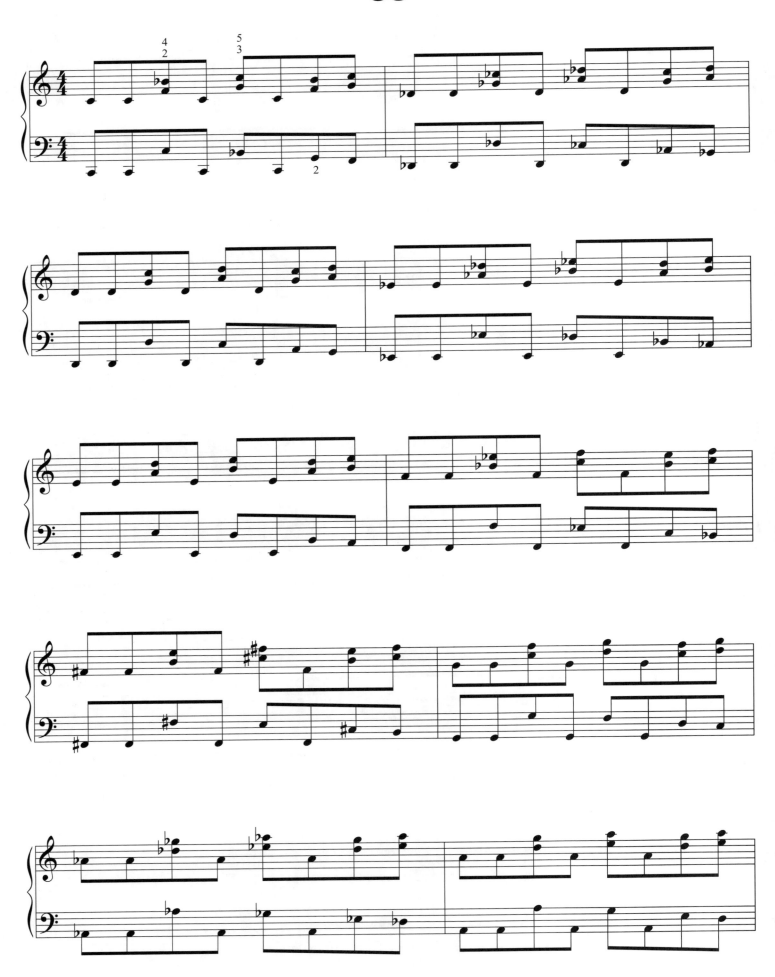

66

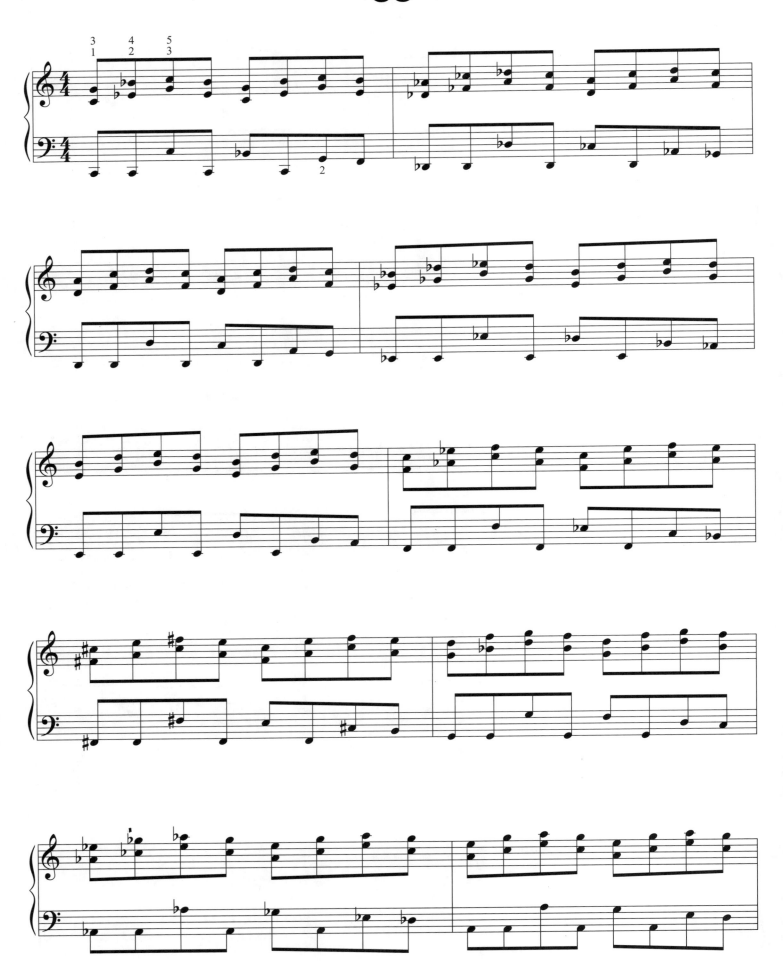

67

68

69

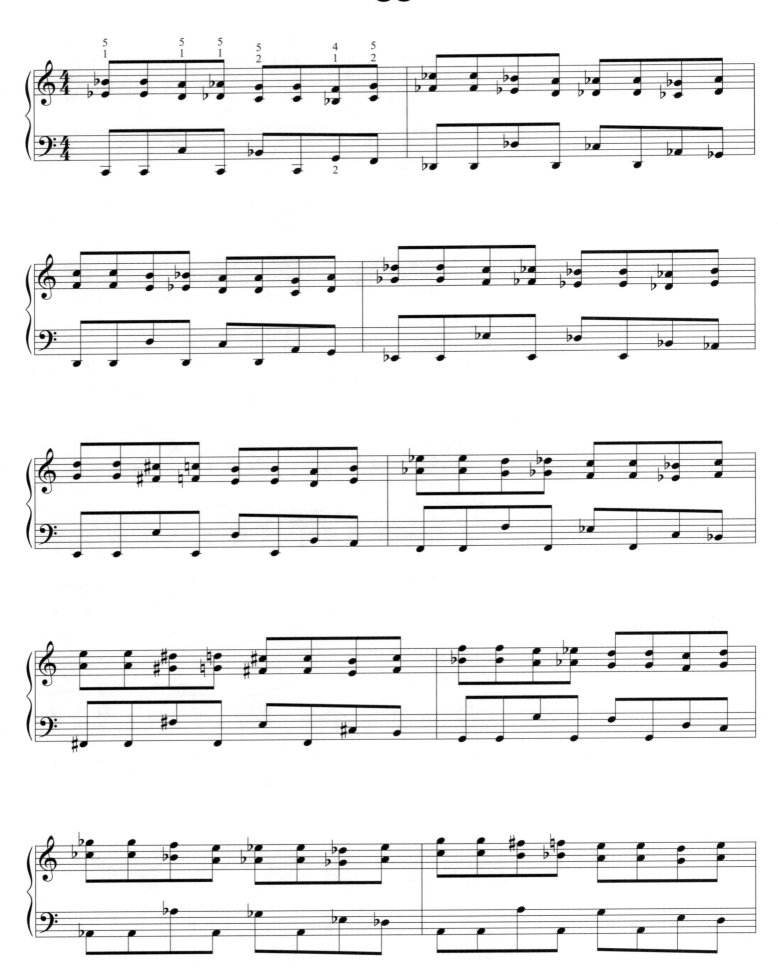

135

70